Meditating
on God's Word

Dr. Aliya Browne

Published by Impresa Book Group

Impresa Books
New Jersey, USA

10 9 8 7 6 5 4 3 2 1

ISBN: 9780990871385 (Paperback)
Printed in The United States of America

Meditating
on God's Word

INTRODUCTION

I started meditating as an adult. Looking back, I realized I was always uneasy or stressed about something moving through life, and hardly ever felt relaxed. As a teen and young adult going to college, medical school, residency and fellowship, and then practicing medicine I had a lot on my plate. My blood pressure increased and it didn't matter what I did in terms of exercise and diet, it stayed elevated and I started medication.

I had a family history of hypertension, so it wasn't unreasonable, but I knew that my levels of stress were also a contributor. When I went into menopause, my hair started falling out, I gained weight and my stress and anxiety levels increased even further. I knew that I had to do something to find some way to cope and to be able to control my stress and anxiety levels and this is how I came across silence and contemplation.

When I discovered stillness and contemplation, I began to initially turn off the radio in the car so that I could have a few moments of silence. Then I started to play praise and worship music in the car in order to silence my mind while thinking of God's goodness. When I started seminary and began learning the different techniques of meditating and contemplation, I realized that the journey of stillness that I had begun years prior were forms of meditation, and that if I added God's words to my regimen of silence I would be able to hide God's words in my heart, be strengthened and be able to use these words to help me along the many journeys towards stillness and strength.

Meditating with God's words using God's scriptures have not only given me tools to use on the battlefield, but it has also strengthened my relationship with God. As I meditated on God's word, I would remember the promises that God gives to each of us. When I was in the middle of the storm. I could recollect what God's word told me, I was strengthened and my stress levels decreased. I could sit in silence and contemplate on the goodness of God without being anxious or stressed or worried. Now I am not saying that I never had stress or anxiety after I started meditating, I am saying that now I had a tool to use to help me in those difficult moments.

Meditating on God's words is not only a tool to use in those difficult moments, but it is also a great way to praise, honor and worship the Lord God. Meditating on God's words in times of joy and happiness only increases that joy and happiness. Meditating on the fruit of the spirit increases those fruits within us and gives us something to look forward to. Meditating on God's love for us increases our love for God because of how great God is. When

I think about the goodness of God and what
God has done for me, my faith increases, my
trust increases and I am grateful and thankful
for all that God is doing in my life.

I encourage you to meditate on God's
words in those moments of need and lack, those
moments of anxiety and depression, and those
moments of joy, peace and happiness. God's
words are true. They are comforting. They never
fail us. Hide God's words within your heart so
that they can minister to you day and night, and
provide comfort and peace when it is needed. I
encourage you incorporate this practice into
your daily life.

WHAT IS MEDITATION?

When you think about meditation, often times the first image you get is that of someone sitting legs crossed, hands out to the knees and eyes closed. Is this the only way to meditate?

Are there any other ways of meditating? Silent contemplation, chants, mindfulness, mantras, what way is the right way? Meditation is "the action or practice of meditating." The origin of this word in Latin is, 'meditari or meditatio;' the act of contemplation, thinking, reflection, studying. It is a way of quieting your mind to truly reflect on your inner spirit and talk with the creator, God. As you quiet your mind you can engage and connect with your spirit and move to an even higher transcendental nature. Meditation causes you to go deeper into your subconscious mind and spirit to obtain a higher appreciation for life.

Meditation can also be a form of prayer.
Contemplating on God's word and allowing one
to go deeper into the meaning of the scriptures
is a form of meditative prayer, contemplation.
There are many forms of meditation, and the
right way is the way that works for you.

There are several types of meditation.
Mindfulness, guided, mantra, focused attention,
and effortless transcending are just a few.
Techniques vary by area, religion, and founders.

Western meditation seeks to train you to
deepen your understanding of the subconscious
mind. Most Western practices of meditation are
linked to God, not just learned as relaxation
techniques. Eastern meditation looks to deepen
one's spiritual mind and self, which leads to
falling into deeper sub-consciousness. Eastern
practices are predominately concerned with the
techniques that lead to deeper transcendental
spaces. Eastern practices may also link with
spirituality and God, but more emphasis is

prominent in Western religious passages such as Christianity, Islam and Judaism. Western practices of meditation, with a God focus, have changed in the past fifty years to be less God focused which has made it more accessible for those who are non-religious.

Mindfulness meditation is being mindful of one's breath, thoughts and feelings, where the goal is to obtain insight in the here and now. Mindfulness meditation seeks to purify and transform your everyday life's circumstances through attaining insight into its bigger picture. Mindfulness meditation is an ancient practice taught by Buddha. Mindfulness means paying attention in a particular way: on purpose, in the present moment, and nonjudgmentally.

All Buddhist meditation aims at the development of awareness, using concentration as a tool toward that end. When you are aware of the moments of your life that you are living in, you begin to live in the present, you begin to attend to the here and now, not living in the past, or living for the future. With the practice of mindfulness, you become aware of who you are. You begin to be and experience life as life happens.

Guided meditation is a meditation technique that assists you in increasing your concentration and awareness. Guided meditation can be religious or non-religious. Chanting a mantra or verse of scripture can guide you along the process towards deeper meditation.

Guided meditations can use words of affirmation, scriptural reference, scan the body for focused areas of awareness or used in forms of imagery. The Hindu tradition of chanting mantras involves repeating different sounds, and or words seeking to improve one's attention, focus and awareness. There are different ways to do mantra meditation. One way is to repeat specific words or sounds that have meaning, another is to just chant a word or sound, but focus specifically on tapping into the minds attention is the main purpose of repeating a mantra.

Mantra meditation is used primarily in the Hindu religion but can also be practiced in Buddhism, Taoism as well as Jainism. The repetition of Om and Shanti are the most basic and common mantras. Mantra meditation should bring your area of concentration to the forefront of your mind, which then produces relaxation, improved focus and a detachment from whatever may be distracting you.

These 21 days we will focus on guided meditation. We will meditate on God's words to bring us more awareness of ourselves and our relationship with God. Meditating on God's word brings these scriptures alive in our everyday lives. These scriptures allow us to think about what God is doing in our lives as it relates to the scripture verse. The scriptures themselves bring enlightenment as the Holy Spirit ministers to us in the stillness. The more you contemplate on the scripture they become a part of you and can be placed in your subconscious mind to provide peace and comfort during trials and tribulations. The scriptures can also provide a sense of joy and anticipation of what God has for us. These guided meditations are meant to provide a foundation and a resource for continued growth in your faith.

WHY MEDITATE

Is it necessary to meditate? If so, why? What are some of the benefits one finds in meditation? There are many reasons why one should meditate. One major purpose of meditation is to gain a deeper awareness of self, one's surroundings, the world, and God. Taking time out of our busy lives to contemplate on God's word and to silence our minds and deepen our spiritual bodies is essential. When you can stop for a second or two to just think about God's goodness and dwell in God's presence it can rejuvenate your entire body and lead to relaxation, reduction of stress and overall improved well being. Another benefit of meditation includes deepening and renewing your physical self. Meditation not only relaxes your mind, but also your body. It can slow your heart rate and keep your blood pressure at normal levels.

Meditation helps bring focus to busy lives and improves concentration and memory. These are just a few things that happen physically, mentally and spiritually. It is beneficial to meditate daily. It's like healing for your entire body.

When you can mentally slow your mind down and contemplate on God's sustaining words you slow down, put a pause on and even erase the busyness, the stress, the anxiety, the depression, as well all the other emotions that you are encountering in the moment. These emotions are replaced with God's words or thoughts. They are replaced with a one word mantra or sentence. They are replaced with stillness. This slows the mind down from racing against the clock. You can either hold on to the joy or hope that you have or run away from the pain or sorrow that you are facing.

Meditation should be something one does

daily. Quieting the mind, becoming aware of your surroundings, your body, your life allows you to live more fully. For many of us we are running along in the rat race, moving from one thing to the next and not being fully aware of what we are leaving behind. We get up, feed ourselves and/or family, go to work, come home and go back to bed. On good days, we may have some meaningful conversations. We may meet some interesting people or have some great interactions. On the many regular days, we may find ourselves getting back into our beds wondering what happened, what was accomplished, and asking ourselves the question of how can I get off this continuously running wheel.

Meditation quiets the mind, and helps you to become aware of what is happening in the here and now, so that you can experience yourself, your life, and just BE. Through heightened awareness brought on in meditation, the spirit and soul are quieted, and a space of knowing and reflection is created. This awareness allows you to slow down and appreciate what's in your surroundings, what's right there, right in front of you. Meditation relaxes not only our inner spirits, but it also relaxes the heart and mind, producing calmness and inner peace.

WHEN TO MEDIATE

Many people meditate first thing in the morning upon waking, some people meditate in the evening to experience and review what happened throughout the day, yet others mediate at specific times set throughout the day. It doesn't matter when you do it, just do it. Meditation is essential to your well being. Some people look at ordinary daily acts as forms of meditation.

Activities such as gardening, praying, listening to worship music, taking a walk in the park, bird watching and even fishing have been thought of as practices of meditation because these activities allow one to focus, contemplate and be aware of the present moment. Whatever it is that allows you to take the time to slow down, contemplate, think and improve your awareness will lead you to a path of stillness and contemplation.

WHERE TO MEDITATE

My favorite places to meditate are in my bed and in my sunroom. Since I like to begin my day with meditation and prayer before my feet hit the floor, I do this before I do anything else. When I wake up late or have so many things on my mind that I jump out of bed and forget my prayers and mediation I notice it in my day.

Some days this prayer and meditation can last 30 to 40 minutes' others it lasts 5 minutes, but whatever it is it is necessary for me to begin each day in this strong way. When I am off from work, or just have a free day, I have a favorite

chair in my sunroom that I will meditate in. As
the sun rises or sets in this room that is full of
orchids and other plants it soothes my soul.

Nature for me allows me to become fully
aware of my surroundings. When I
contemplate, and think about my day, quieting
my mind and thinking about God's presence in
my life in that room, I can feel the presence of
God. I can feel God in the stillness. Sometimes
while walking in the woods I will practice my
breathing, quiet my mind and bring awareness
to my surroundings; practicing walking
meditation. Other places I've meditated include
the beach, the library, really, just about any
place.

I will practice a meditative prayer to calm
my nerves before doing something I'm anxious
or stressed about. When I'm at my desk and I
have just heard some bad news, or things aren't
going my way, I'll take a moment, focus my
breathing and meditate on a favorite scripture

that calms me. Meditation can be practiced anywhere, even on a crowded subway. Meditation is heightened awareness, contemplation, thinking; that can be done anywhere you are. So, the most important thing to do is to find that place that relaxes you and start there. It may be the floor in your prayer closet. It may be sitting at your dining room table. It may be, like for me, lying in bed first thing in the morning. Wherever it is, just get to it, and make it a habit.

HOW TO MEDITATE

You can't force it!

Things to think of before you even sit down crossed legged, in your chair or in your bed... don't expect for this to be an Ah-Ha moment, or that you'll see results the first moment you sit and quiet your mind. When you start this new process, begin with an open mind prepared for whatever happens, because it will happen in its own way.

Don't sit down and attempt to make something happen, or over analyze what is happening. You're doing it right. Believe me. Relax, release and respond to your body's signals. Be kind to yourself as you travel along in the process. The most important thing is to just BE in the moment, feel what is happening, and relax into it.

Once ready to begin, the first exercise to consider perfecting is your breathing. Most people never take a full breath, as many people are shallow breathers. Breathing is essential and most of us never think about how we are breathing we just breathe. If you're female and or overly conscious about your waistline many times you're sucking that gut in which does not allow for a full inspiration. Breathing is essential. Have you ever noticed that there are times when you are prepared to give that speech, or talk with that difficult client, by the time you are there you feel like you are going to pass out? That may happen because you've not been fully breathing. You've worked yourself up so much that your breathing is even shallower than it normally is, and you don't even realize it. You've not breathed deeply for so long in your life that when it's essential, you fail to even realize that you need to deepen your breathing.

Deeper breathing. Why is that so

important? Taking a deep breath is important because when you don't fully inhale and exhale your oxygen levels decrease and the body goes into oxygen crave mode. The low levels of oxygen leave our organs depleted and our blood levels drop. Our body will then increase our breathing so that we take in more oxygen. This produces shallower breathing. Toxins are released when we breathe deeply and when we don't they build up within our bodies. Over time these toxins build up within our organs. When we breathe shallowly we are releasing too much carbon dioxide and the PH in our bodies increases. This increase causes our bodies to not function appropriately, and it leads to symptoms of tingling, confusion and lightheadedness, sure signs of oxygen depletion. Learning how to deep breathe improves the function of our bodies to become fully oxygenated and feed our organs oxygen, which we desperately need. We must breathe deeply to allow these chemicals to be in balance in our lives. Carbon dioxide is an essential molecule and is a natural waste product in our breathing and oxygen is essential to our entire bodies, but when we don't breathe deeply the decrease in the carbon dioxide and oxygen wreaks havoc on our bodies. Through learning how to breathe in meditation, with focused awareness on the breath and with controlling your breath, you will improve oxygenation to all your organs: heart, brain, lungs, liver etc. This is essential to living well.

Some people use beads as a reminder during their meditations. Roman Catholics, Orthodox Christians, Muslims, Buddhist and Hindu religions all have prayer beads that assist their followers in their prayers of meditation and contemplation.

The Catholic rosary has five stations, depending on what they are praying and mediating on will be how many times you go around the string of beads. Buddhist and Hindu beads allow one to count the mantra during meditative prayers as does Orthodox Christian prayer beads. They all usher the meditator to face focused awareness of prayers as they meditate around the beads. Beads are great tools to use during meditation. They are a constant reminder to be aware and bring ones focus back to whatever is being contemplated.

LET'S GET STARTED

This 21-day guided meditation and introduction to meditating with God's word will guide you into a deeper relationship with God. Each week we will meditate on one topic. The memory/meditation verses will be hidden inside your heart so that as you meditate on them they become a part of you. Each day as they become a part of you, they can be used as tools along your Christian walk. These tools can be used to help strengthen and guide you.

As the scriptures become embedded into your heart and mind your faith in God will deepen and they will provide answers, comfort and meaning along your Christian walk. The longer you meditate on scripture they are set to memory so that when you are in situations where you need a word of encouragement, or you need to give a word of encouragement it is already in your data bank ready for you to make a withdrawal.

Each week we will focus on a different topic: Week 1- Health, Week 2- Wealth, Week 3- Family

These areas, individually, are great ways to focus on your life, and combined they are a force to be reckoned with. Each week as we meditate we will meditate on scriptures concerning the focused area.

The first week, if you are a beginner, you will spend 5 minutes on the meditation and scripture. The second week you will increase the time to 10 minutes with longer passages and scriptures to meditate on. The third week time will be increased to 15 minutes.

The focus here will be to deepen the connection with your breath as well as lengthen the time of focusing on the scriptural passages.

As you do each guided meditation, capture your thoughts in the space provided answering the questions of -reflections and final thoughts.

As you go along in your day you will be attentive to what quieting your mind brings, and reflect on what the scripture means to you. If you are not a beginner feel free to begin your meditation as you normally would and then spend as much time as you normally do on the guided meditation.

After this 21 day kick off, I encourage you to go back to the first week and meditate on the scriptures provided for 20 minutes and keep going through these weeks until you can increase your time to whatever you feel best, preferably at or more than 30 minutes. Studies have shown that 27 minutes of daily meditation can alter your brains chemistry, and improve your underlying capacity for learning and memory, compassion and self-awareness. You will be amazed at how your overall wellness will improve as you incorporate this daily meditative practice into your life; mind, body and spirit.

So, lets' get to it....

WEEK 1: HEALTH

Your health is your wealth is a common slogan that has evolved over the past few years.

One of the reasons why this has evolved is because studies have shown that the wealthiest people are some of the healthiest people. They eat better, they exercise and their overall quality of life appears to be better, but don't let this fool you. The lives of the wealthiest people can also be some of the most stressful. When we invest in our health we live longer.

Maintaining your health is the most important thing you can do to live longer, healthy, fulfilled lives. The more we invest in our health through diet, exercise, healthy eating and improving our mental and spiritual bodies with prayer, fasting and meditation the longer we live stronger wealthier lives. Now, I am not talking about monetary wealth. I am talking about wealth as it relates to your well being, wholeness, and abundance of life. Your health is your wealth. Meditation can improve your health through quieting the mind, deepening the spirit, improving your stress and anxiety levels and improving your overall well being.

Each day before you begin, find a quiet space and get into a position that relaxes you enough to concentrate on meditating, but doesn't put you to sleep. I like meditating in my bed first thing in the morning. I am still and relaxed and if I am fully awake I can stay there and meditate. Sometimes if I am tired and have not fully awakened, I find that I will fall in and out of sleep and meditation. When this happens, I get up and onto my meditation pillow so I can fully participate in the state of meditation. There are many others that meditate while sitting in a comfy chair, or meditate by going to their favorite outdoors location. Do whatever works for you. Once you've found your place and you are ready to begin, zone in on your breathing and take a few deep breaths before beginning your guided meditation.

One form of focused breathing is 4/7/8 breathing developed by Dr. Andrew Weil, MD. The technique is described below:

"Although you can do the exercise in any position, sit with your back straight while learning the exercise. Place the tip of your tongue against the ridge of tissue just behind your upper front teeth, and keep it there through the entire exercise. You will be exhaling through your mouth around your tongue; try pursing your lips slightly if this seems awkward.

Exhale completely through your mouth, making a whoosh sound.

Close your mouth and inhale quietly through your nose to a mental count of four.

Hold your breath for a count of seven.

Exhale completely through your mouth,

making a whoosh sound to a count of eight.
*   This is one breath.*
*   Now inhale again and repeat the cycle*
three more times for a total of four breaths."

 Now you're ready. You've focused on your breathing and you can now be guided through God's word in meditation.

This first week you will meditate on the scripture for 5 minutes. Read the scripture say it over and over in your head, while deep breathing. It's okay if your mind wanders to other thoughts, and it will, welcome these thoughts in and then usher them out of your mind as you continue to meditate. Since you're meditating on scriptures that may not be memorized it's okay to keep your eyes opened. Closed eyes are not a prerequisite to meditation.

Namaste is a typical closing for many forms of meditation. Namaste is a greeting that means in Hindi, "I bow to the divine in you." It is a greeting that acknowledges that the divine is within each of us. When one says this, one's hands are placed at the level of the heart chakra. In all actuality, you don't even have to say the words in some circles, just placing the hands at the level of the heart chakra and bowing, bows to the divine in the other.

I always end my meditations with John 14:27 which says, *"Peace I leave with you, my peace I give you."*

Go in peace. We all want God's peace, this peace that surpasses all understanding. I end with this peace offering to God from all of us, so that God's peace can dwell within each of us.

The divine is in each of us, and we usher in the divines, God's, peace, into ourselves at the end of our meditation. I truly believe that meditation is a form of prayer, and so most of my meditations will end with an AMEN. Amen being a standard ending to a prayer. Amen, Yes, or so be it is a great way to end a meditation.

DAY 1: *Be Still And Know*

Stillness is a way to conquer your mind. In the stillness, you find peace and tranquility. Being still means that all is halted. Time stops. You can consciously be awake and aware of all that is going on in your body. Stillness is a state of alerted attention to what is right now in the moment. In this moment, we are knowing that God is the great I AM. Be still and know that I AM is God. Be still and know that the I AM is God and will be exalted in all the nations in all the earth. Be still and know that I AM God reminds us of who God is and all that God is for and to us.

Focus on the Word emphasized and then
Repeat.
Take a Deep Breath.
Get into a comfortable position.
Breathe In through your nose for 4 counts.
Hold for 7 counts.
Breathe through your mouth for 8 counts.
Repeat 3 times.

Psalm 46:10 NIV

*"Be still and know that I am God; I will be
exalted among the nations; I will be exalted in
the earth."*

Be still and know that I am God.
Be still and know that I am God.
Be still and know that I am God.
Be still and know that I am God.
Be. Still. Know. God.
Be Still and Know that I am God. Be Still.
Know God. Be.

Peace I leave with you. My peace I give you. Go
in peace. Amen.

Reflections and Final Thoughts

_____

_____

_____

_____

_____

DAY 2: *A Psalm of David*

The 23rd Psalm is a psalm of David. It is probably the most well known psalm in the Bible. This is a prayer for protection. In this psalm the psalter acknowledges that the Lord is the shepherd of their life.

The Lord has led them and refreshed them and tended to their every need. The Lord has walked with them even in the still and quiet of the day when all is well, but also has lead them in the darkest of valleys. God's love for the psalter has been a sustaining force in their life, and so too will the Lord be a sustaining force in our lives as well.

This is a great psalm to meditate on day and night. This week as we think about and contemplate on our health we can meditate on Psalm 23, which reminds us that our God will sustain us in all circumstances, both good and bad.

As we meditate, contemplating and ushering in good health we know that even in those darkest moments when we may be waiting to hear from the doctors, or even hospitalized we can be sure to see that the Lord's rod and staff will give us comfort in the storm.

Take a Deep Breath.
Get into a comfortable position.
Breathe In through your nose for 4 counts.
Hold for 7 counts.
Breathe through your mouth for 8 counts.
Repeat 3 times.

Psalm 23

The Lord is my shepherd, I lack nothing.

He makes me lie down in green pastures, he leads me beside quiet waters,

he refreshes my soul. He guides me along the right paths for his name's sake.

Even though I walk through the darkest valley, I will fear no evil, for you are with me;

your rod and your staff, they comfort me.

You prepare a table before me in the presence of my enemies. You anoint my head with oil; my cup overflows. Surely your goodness and love will follow me all the days of my life, and I will dwell in the house of the Lord Forever.

Peace I leave with you. My peace I give you.
Go in peace. Amen.

Reflections and Final Thoughts

_____

_____

_____

_____

_____

DAY 3: *Praise the Lord*

Praising the Lord is an essential part of the daily Christian walk. When we praise God, we let God know that we love God and we thank God for all the many miracles big and small.

Meditation can be a form of praise. When we praise God through meditation we thank God for the many times he has hearkened God's ear to our cries. When we meditate on God's scriptures as a form of worship we are honoring God for all of who God is.

When our meditation is a form of worship we praise and adore God for keeping us healthy, and healing our bodies, minds and spirit. The psalmist writes praise the Lord, my soul and all my inmost being, praise his holy name.

When we meditate on the holy name of God we praise God for God's holiness, righteousness and forgiving power that heals us.

Take a Deep Breath.

Get into a comfortable position.

Breathe In through your nose for 4 counts.

Hold for 7 counts.

Breathe through your mouth for 8 counts.

Repeat 3 times.

Psalm 103:1-5

"Praise the Lord, my soul; all my inmost being, praise his holy name. Praise the Lord, my soul, and forget not all his benefits— who forgives all your sins and heals all your diseases, who redeems your life from the pit and crowns you with love and compassion, who satisfies your desires with good things so that your youth is renewed like the eagle's."

Praise the LORD, oh my Soul and all that is
within me. Praise God's holy name.
Peace I leave with you, My peace I give you.
Go in Peace. Amen

Reflections and Final Thoughts

_____

_____

_____

_____

_____

DAY 4: *Jesus Is A Healer*

The passage here in the book of Isaiah
foretells the coming of our LORD Jesus Christ.
Isaiah speaks of Jesus' crucifixion and suffering
to bear the sins of the world, to heal the world.
Isaiah first begins with asking the question of
belief. Do you believe the scriptures? Do you
believe the stories of God to be true?

God has revealed God's self to God's
people. God revealed how Jesus could come to
the earth without much fanfare majesty or
anything to attract himself to the people. Jesus
would be despised and rejected and would
suffer and feel pain, but ultimately Jesus would
take away our pain, suffering and afflictions to
bring peace and healing to the world.

Because of Jesus's suffering we can be

assured that we are saved and healed. Jesus brought peace and healing to the world, meditating on these things brings peace and healing to all of us.

Take a Deep Breath.
Get into a comfortable position.
Breathe In through your nose for 4 counts.
Hold for 7 counts.
Breathe through your mouth for 8 counts.
Repeat 3 times.

Isaiah 53:1-5

"Who has believed our message and to whom has the arm of the Lord been revealed? He grew up before him like a tender shoot, and like a root out of dry ground. He had no beauty or majesty to attract us to him, nothing in his appearance that we should desire him. He was despised and rejected by mankind, a man of suffering, and familiar with pain. Like one from whom people hide their faces he was despised, and we held him in low esteem. Surely he took up our pain and bore our suffering, yet we considered him punished by God, stricken by him, and afflicted. But he was pierced for our transgressions, he was crushed for our iniquities; the punishment that brought us peace was on him, and by his wounds we are healed."

Peace I leave with you, My peace I give you.

Go in Peace. Amen

Reflections and Final Thoughts

_____

_____

_____

_____

_____

DAY 5: *God's Love for You*

Children learn in Sunday school that well studied verse *"For God so loved the world that he gave his one and only Son, that whoever believes in him shall not perish but have eternal life."* (John 3:16)

God's love for us, God's children, is deeper than any love out there. God loves us so much that God sent Jesus to save us and bring us into his own. This passage reminds us that God will be with us, each believer, blessing us and loving us as any parent would do. However, we do have the responsibility of obeying and following God.

When we obey, and follow God, God will bless us beyond what we can imagine. God will increase our numbers on the job, in the house, as well as in the nation. We shall prosper and be healthy without sickness or disease. God promises these things to all those who follow

God's words, and forget not the benefits of belief.

Take a Deep Breath.

Get into a comfortable position.

Breathe In through your nose for 4 counts.

Hold for 7 counts.

Breathe through your mouth for 8 counts.

Repeat 3 times.

Deuteronomy 7:12-16

"If you pay attention to these laws and are careful to follow them, then the Lord your God will keep his covenant of love with you, as he swore to your ancestors. He will love you and bless you and increase your numbers. He will bless the fruit of your womb, the crops of your land —your grain, new wine and olive oil— the calves of your herds and the lambs of your flocks in the land he swore to your ancestors to give you. You will be blessed more than any other people; none of your men or women will be childless, nor will any of your livestock be without young. The Lord will keep you free from every disease. He will not inflict on you the horrible diseases you knew in Egypt, but he will inflict them on all who hate you. You must destroy all the peoples the Lord your God gives over to you. Do not look on them with pity and do not serve their gods, for that will be a snare to you."

Peace I leave with you, My peace I give you. Go
in Peace. Amen

Reflections and Final Thoughts

_____

_____

_____

_____

_____

DAY 6: *Loving God's Word*

The reading, studying and memorization of God's word is essential for one's health. Hiding God's words within our hearts gives us the tools we need to be healthy. Paying attention to God's word, turning our ears to the words of God and reading it every day keeps the word of God within our hearts, souls, and minds.

God's words bring life to the soul and our entire body. Essential to reading the word of God and meditating on God's word is keeping these words within your heart and mind. Keeping these words of God helps us to guard our hearts each day from the ways of the world.

When God's word is hidden in your heart it flows out of everything you do. Memorizing God's word gives us the tools we need to fight against the principalities of this world. The proverb tells us to never let God's word out of our sight, that's our spiritual eye. The scriptures

must be hidden within our hearts and minds.
God's words are healing to our entire bodies.

Take a Deep Breath.

Get into a comfortable position.

Breathe In through your nose for 4 counts.

Hold for 7 counts.

Breathe through your mouth for 8 counts.

Repeat 3 times.

Proverbs 4:20-23

"My son, pay attention to what I say; turn your ear to my words. Do not let them out of your sight, keep them within your heart; for they are life to those who find them and health to one's whole body. Above all else, guard your heart, for everything you do flows from it."

Peace I leave with you, My peace I give you.
Go in Peace. Amen

Reflections and Final Thoughts

_____

_____

_____

_____

_____

DAY 7: *Intercessory Prayer*

To be an intercessor for someone means to stand in the gap. Standing in the gap and taking your petitions on behalf of someone else is a powerful form of prayer. When we truly stand in the gap for another and love our neighbors as ourselves as Jesus Christ instructed us to do, then we are truly being obedient to the word of God. We are truly living out this meditation in our everyday lives.

Many people ask for and are asked each day to make petition to God for the other. Intercessory prayer is important because we all can then think of, contemplate on and cherish the concerns of one another. When our family and friends need intercession, we can also meditate on God's word on behalf of them.

This passage in John reminds us that it is our job to ask others, more specifically the elders of the church to make intercession on our behalf. This verse is important to me not only because of this reminder, but also because it reminds me that when my faith is strong I will be made whole, I will be well, and my sins will be forgiven. It also reminds all of us that we must confess our sins one to another during this process of healing so that we can be healed.

When we pray with righteous faith-filled strong believers, our prayers are powerful and effective. The more we bring our petitions to God, and the elders of the church, those faithful servants of God, the stronger we become, and we will be healed.

Take a Deep Breath.
Get into a comfortable position.
Breathe In through your nose for 4 counts.
Hold for 7 counts.
Breathe through your mouth for 8 counts.
Repeat 3 times.

James 5:13-16

"Is anyone among you in trouble? Let them pray. Is anyone happy? Let them sing songs of praise. Is anyone among you sick? Let them call the elders of the church to pray over them and anoint them with oil in the name of the Lord. And the prayer offered in faith will make the sick person well; the Lord will raise them up. If they have sinned, they will be forgiven. Therefore confess your sins to each other and pray for each other so that you may be healed."

Peace I leave with you. My peace I give you. Go in peace. Amen.

Reflections and Final Thoughts

_____

_____

_____

_____

_____

WEEK 2: WEALTH

This week we will be focusing on our wealth. As we meditate on our wealth we will be targeting three areas of wealth; physical, mental and spiritual wealth. Some of the wealthiest people I know have little monetary, or physical wealth. When people think of and hear the word "wealth", or "wealthy" many times the first thing that comes to mind is monetary wealth, but monetary and/or physical wealth is not the only type of wealth there is. Wealth, as defined by Merriam-Webster's dictionary is the "abundance of valuable material possessions or resources."

A secondary definition is abundant supply, and or "a plentiful supply of a particular valuable thing". Wealth can be anything that supplies value to our lives.

Physical/Monetary Wealth is what we possess either through purchasing, gifting or inheritance. This physical/monetary wealth is dependent on what we acquire through work or through family. Mental Wealth can be defined as "an amount of developmental knowledge and wisdom of which one has contributed their efforts into obtaining over the course of their life, thus far. It is the total sum of useable knowledge which can be applied into one's life for the benefit of prosperity."(christopherpicardi.com)

This mental wealth is created by the persistent desire to learn more in a 'plentiful supply.' Spiritual wealth is that plentiful supply of grace that God gives to every believer. This spiritual wealth is also dependent on the work that we do to develop it and grow closer to God through one's faith.

As we meditate on God's scripture concerning our wealth this week we will be practicing these meditations from a holistic point of view. We will be meditating on improving our wealth from a spiritual, physical and mental perspective. When one thinks about one's life from a holistic perspective then one can concentrate on seeking God for all things in life. Holistic living means seeking God's direction in all aspects of one's life.

This week we will be meditating on the scripture passages for a total of 10 minutes.

Start off with your breathing exercise. After your breathing exercise read the scripture. As you read it, think about its meaning to you and pick out words that stand out for you. Continue to re-read the scripture and meditate on its meaning in your life. After your time is up end with your peace scripture and Amen.

Let us begin Week 2.

Day 1: *Wealth & Blessings*

A well-known prayer passage is the Prayer
of Jabez. The bible tells us that he was most
honored amongst his siblings. He was a praying
man and when he prayed to God he was focused
on his wealth, not only his physical wealth but
also his spiritual and mental wealth. In this
short prayer sent up to God by Jabez, Jabez
asks to be blessed, that he will have more
wealth and responsibility, that he will grow in
spiritual wealth and that God will protect him,
which can also include his mental health. Jabez
covered all his bases here in this prayer. Two
sentences and God granted his request. Many
times, we pray and are long winded and never
get down to the specifics. Here Jabez sums of all
he needs in two short sentences and God
blesses him.

Sometimes, less is more. Jabez's prayer

reveals that to all of us. Lord bless me means
Lord increase my physical, mental and
emotional wealth so that I can do your will.
Increase my territory means give me more than
I have right now, give me more wealth, more
responsibility, more. Let your hand be with me-
never leave me nor forsake me, help me and
stay with me along the way- increase my
spiritual and mental wealth. Lord God keep me
from harm and free from pain- increase my
mental and physical (bodily) wealth, keep me
protected and healthy along the way. As we
meditate on this Prayer from Jabez, let us focus
on increasing our entire bodies wealth;
physical, mental and spiritual.

Take a Deep Breath.

Get into a comfortable position.

Breathe In through your nose for 4 counts.

Hold for 7 counts.

Breathe out through your mouth for 8 counts.

Repeat 3 times.

Chronicles 4:10

"Jabez cried out to the God of Israel, "Oh that you would bless me and enlarge my territory! Let your hand be with me, and keep me from harm so that I will be free from pain." And God granted his request."

Peace I leave with you.

My peace I give you. Go in peace. Amen.

Reflections and Final Thoughts

_____

_____

_____

_____

_____

Day 2: *Get Wisdom*

Mental wealth, the ability to take in all that
the world offers through education and seeking
God's direction and purpose for one's life. When
you are mentally wealthy you seek after God
and pay attention to God's word. God teaches us
the ways of the world each day. If only we'd take
heed and pay attention, not forsaking what God
has in store for us. When we take hold of God's
word and keep God's commandments, and hide
God's word in our hearts to never sin against
God we grow in mental wealth. This mental
wealth gives us wisdom and understanding,
God's understanding. When we seek wisdom, it
won't forsake us. When we are wise according
to God's words we will be protected from the
world. Wisdom does not come cheap, wisdom is
expensive and costs us all we have because we
must let ourselves go and trust in God, but to
gain wisdom we must be wise enough to follow

God. Get wisdom, get understanding, because it
is all we have for mental wealth.

Take a Deep Breath.

Get into a comfortable position.

Breathe In through your nose for 4 counts.

Hold for 7 counts.

Breathe out through your mouth for 8 counts.

Repeat 3 times.

Proverbs 4:1-7

Listen, my sons, to a father's instruction; pay attention and gain understanding. I give you sound learning, so do not forsake my teaching. For I too was a son to my father, still tender, and cherished by my mother. Then he taught me, and he said to me, "Take hold of my words with all your heart; keep my commands, and you will live. Get wisdom, get understanding; do not forget my words or turn away from them. Do not forsake wisdom, and she will protect you; love her, and she will watch over you. The beginning of wisdom is this: Get wisdom. Though it cost all you have, get understanding.

Peace I leave with you. My peace I give you. Go in Peace. Amen.

Reflections and Final Thoughts

_____

_____

_____

_____

_____

Day 3: *Trust God*

To gain any wealth, spiritual-mental- or physical, you must trust in God. Trusting God is so important in seeking wealth. Trusting God means believing with every morsel in your body that God's word is true, reliable and strong. Trusting God means that you have full confidence in what God says, God will do. Trusting God with all our heart mind and soul and not thinking about or leaning on our own understanding but acknowledging that God's way is the only way guides us on our journey to wealth. Trusting God means that we are following God's wisdom and honoring God in all that we do. Fear of the Lord is our strength, when we fear God and revere God we will not only be physically healthy and wealthy but we will be spiritually healthy because God provides all our nourishment. We honor God for all God does by giving back to God the 'first fruits' of all our crops. That means not only monetary giving, but also spiritual and mental giving. Honor God by worshipping and praising him with the best of ourselves. Honor God by studying Gods word, and rising early in the morning to spend time with God mediating and giving God our first fruits of attention. When we honor God with our best, God then honors us with God's best, more than we could ever earn ourselves. Trust God, honor God and God will increase our wealth.

Take a Deep Breath.
Get into a comfortable position.
Breathe In through your nose for 4 counts.
Hold for 7 counts.
Breathe out through your mouth for 8 counts.
Repeat 3 times.

Proverbs 3:5-10

Trust in the Lord with all your heart and lean not on your own understanding; in all your ways submit to him, and he will make your paths straight. Do not be wise in your own eyes; fear the Lord and shun evil. This will bring health to your body and nourishment to your bones. Honor the Lord with your wealth, with the first fruits of all your crops; then your barns will be filled to overflowing, and your vats will brim over with new wine.

Peace I leave with you. My peace I give you. Go in Peace. Amen.

Reflections and Final Thoughts

_____

_____

_____

_____

_____

Day 4: *Power*

God's power runs deep in every believer; we just must tap into it. God's power gives us the ability to move mountains. God's power provides us with all that we need, and some of our wants.

The power of God casts away all fears, doubts, and worries, and replaces them with mental wealth and prosperity. God has not given us the spirit of fear; God casts out all fear. God gives each of us power, love and self-discipline. This self-discipline, or sound mind, helps us to build up the mental wealth that will sustain us and help us to be able to accomplish and acquire all that God has in store for us, what God has already prepared for us to have and to do.

God is all powerful and when we tap into that power, just like the woman with the issue of blood who just tapped on to God's hem, we too can be healed and transformed, and made whole again.

We should never be ashamed of what God does for us. When God blesses us with wealth we should shout on high God's praises. When we are suffering for what we know is right we should shout on high God's praises.

God has saved us and set us apart and made us holy in God's sight. God has given us God's grace, love and mercy and power, because God loves us. God's love for us has destroyed deaths sting and has given us life and immortality; now that's powerful.

Take a Deep Breath.

Get into a comfortable position.

Breathe In through your nose for 4 counts.

Hold for 7 counts.

Breathe out through your mouth for 8 counts.

Repeat 3 times.

Timothy 1:6-10

For this reason I remind you to fan into flame the gift of God, which is in you through the laying on of my hands. For the Spirit God gave us does not make us timid, but gives us power, love and self-discipline. So do not be ashamed of the testimony about our Lord or of me his prisoner. Rather, join with me in suffering for the gospel, by the power of God. He has saved us and called us to a holy life— not because of anything we have done but because of his own purpose and grace. This grace was given us in Christ Jesus before the beginning of time, but it has now been revealed through the appearing of our Savior, Christ Jesus, who has destroyed death and has brought life and immortality to light through the gospel.

Peace I leave with you. My peace I give you. Go in peace. Amen.

Reflections and Final Thoughts

_____

_____

_____

_____

_____

Day 5: *Obedience*

Wealthy people tend to follow some directions, some laws. To be wealthy, and not only have inherited it, some work must be done. Whether its studying hard in school or following the markets, having a great idea or having God driven talent, to stay wealthy one must get in the game and do something. Maintaining our physical, mental and spiritual wealth not only means investing in ourselves through studying and perfecting our techniques, but it also means seeking God's will for our lives through prayer, fasting, and studying the word of God.

When we read the word of God we not only learn more about the stories of God, but we also gain the tools we need that help us to be able to do the work of God, the work and assignment God has given to each of us.

As we meditate on scriptures and
memorize the decrees of God we grow stronger
in our faith. The word of the Lord will
strengthen us; it will help us to be able to fight
the good fight. It will give us joy in the good
times and the bad times. It instructs us and
becomes the tools we need to lead a life filled
with love, joy and peace.

The word of God guides our path; it lights
the road we travel. Just like the deer pants after
water, we shall pant and thirst after the word of
God, but not only pant after it, we shall follow it
all the days of our lives. God's word sometimes
convicts us, it draws us closer to him, it reveals
to us our faults as well as our strengths. The
more we study it, the stronger we become in our
faith in Christ.

These 21 days, as we pray, as we meditate
on these scriptures remember 1 Peter 2:1-3,
reminds us that when we study the word of
God, God lights our paths and leads us down

the paths of righteousness for God's names
sake. Continue to follow the light of God,
continue to thirst after God's word, and
continue to obey the Lord's decrees. God will
reveal Gods-self to you and make your paths
straight

Take a Deep Breath.
Get into a comfortable position.
Breathe In through your nose for 4 counts.
Hold for 7 counts.
Breathe out through your mouth for 8 counts.
Repeat 3 times.

Psalm 119:103-106

*How sweet are your words to my taste,
sweeter than honey to my mouth! I gain
understanding from your precepts; therefore I
hate every wrong path. Your word is a lamp
for my feet, a light on my path. I have taken an
oath and confirmed it, that I will follow your
righteous laws.*

Peace I leave with you. My peace I give you.
Go in Peace. Amen

Reflections and Final Thoughts

_____

_____

_____

_____

_____

Day 6: *God is ALL things*

Our God, our Lord, our Savior. Jehovah Jirah, Jehovah Nissi, Jehovah Rapha. Elohim, El Shaddai. Abba Father. Our God is all things. Our God is all powerful. Our God has many names because our God is we are. We are from God, and through God and for God, we are who we are because of God. The Lord God almighty is a great and mighty God. God is the author and finisher of all things. God's wisdom and knowledge is from everlasting to everlasting and we could never imagine, think of or know all of who God is. It's impossible. God is unsearchable.

When we think about God's goodness, and mercy, and love, and grace we glorify God's name for these gifts that God has given unto us. All glory honor and praise are due to our Lord and Savior Jesus Christ. To him be the glory forever. God is all things and this means that

God has all things, and can increase our wealth in all areas of life. God has many names because God is all powerful and is able to do all things and provide all things exceedingly and abundantly above anything that we could even imagine.

Take a Deep Breath.
Get into a comfortable position.
Breathe In through your nose for 4 counts.
Hold for 7 counts.
Breathe out through your mouth for 8 counts.
Repeat 3 times.

Romans 11:33-36

Oh, the depth of the riches of the wisdom and knowledge of God! How unsearchable his judgments, and his paths beyond tracing out! "Who has known the mind of the Lord? Or who has been his counselor?" "Who has ever given to God, that God should repay them?" For from him and through him and for him are all things. To him be the glory forever! Amen.

Peace I leave with you. My peace I give you. Go in Peace. Amen

Reflections and Final Thoughts

_____

_____

_____

_____

_____

Day 7: *Relationship*

Every good leader and most wealthy people
know that you can't do it alone. When we only
strive to better ourselves and never think about
others we cannot see and receive all that God
has for us. Having relationship and community
is tantamount to having great wealth.

We may have all heard about the wealthy
person who doesn't share, doesn't have
relationships or community and suddenly finds
themselves wishing they could give it all back
because they are so lonely.

Being wealthy means that we share in the
bounty that God has given to us. It means that
we share in the blessings that God has given to
us. It means that we are one in spirit and mind
with our brothers and sisters in Christ who are
in need.

When God blesses us with physical, mental
and spiritual wealth we must share what we

have with others. This is how we will receive the ultimate blessings from God. Being there for one another in community and in relationship is the greatest gift we can give ourselves. When we do this, we are truly exemplifying Gods qualities of love, faith and humility.

When we value others interests as much as or even more than our own then we are truly humbling ourselves to Gods wishes and desires in our lives and we can truly build up and increase our own spiritual, mental and emotional wealth.

Thanks be to God for community and relationships and the ability to build wealth just by being in community with others.

Take a Deep Breath.
Get into a comfortable position.

Breathe In through your nose for 4 counts.

Hold for 7 counts.

Breathe out through your mouth for 8 counts.

Repeat 3 times.

Philippians 2:1-4

Therefore if you have any encouragement from being united with Christ, if any comfort from his love, if any common sharing in the Spirit, if any tenderness and compassion, then make my joy complete by being like-minded, having the same love, being one in spirit and of one mind. Do nothing out of selfish ambition or vain conceit. Rather, in humility value others above yourselves, not looking to your own interest but each of you to the interests of the others.

Peace I leave with you. My peace I give you.
Go in Peace. AMEN

Reflections and Final Thoughts

_____

_____

_____

_____

_____

WEEK 3: FAMILY

This last week we will be focusing on the family. We've all heard and some of us may even say that colloquial term "Family First," even watched the program Focus on the Family. Well we should put our families first, we should focus on our families.

Many times we do put our families first, that is first before everything else, but does God tell us that having a healthy family means putting our family first above all things. Family first doesn't always mean though putting our families first; first before everything. SO, what does it mean to have a family? What does God's word tell us about family? What is the importance of family in the bible, and how can we emulate God's word in our families? Why should we even consider putting our families first and why is it even so important to consider this?

Let's look to our first family Adam and Eve.

God created Eve because God knew the importance of family. God saw that Adam was alone and needed family and so Eve was created to be that family for Adam. With Adam and Eve as the first family they could live, trust, work together, follow God and love one another unconditionally. The bible tells us they were naked and unashamed. This means in every aspect of their bodies, mind, body and spirit, they were interconnected. They shared everything. They were equal partners, with God as the head, leading them and guiding them along the way.

As we can see from the fall they did everything together. I'm not saying that was the best decision, but they supported one another when Eve talked with the serpent and then eventually ate the fruit Adam was right there by her side.

When she gave it to Adam to eat, he shared in the responsibility of their actions. Here was their biggest mistake in my opinion and the opinion of many others, they put their family first, not God. God had said not to eat of the fruit in the center of the garden, they both knew it, but they both disobeyed God. God must be put first in our families, then the family.

This week we will meditate on scriptures about our families, and focus on how we can put God first in our families to have healthy, strong families dedicated completely to God. As we meditate on scriptures regarding our families this week as in all our weeks we will continue to focus on having holistic healthy families. Improving our families physical mental and spiritual health will therefore be the focus.

Day 1: *Productivity*

God has given each of us an assignment. Sometimes these assignments run in families. We all know some families where everyone is musically talented, singers, dancers, performers. Some families are brains all engineers, lawyers, doctors. The Levites were all called to be priests. Some families, like Jesus' family were called to be great carpenters and others like David, Solomon and Saul great leaders. We all have an assignment from God and when we are born into these families we must find out what our collective/family assignment is, as well as what our individual assignments will be.

God gives to each of us the tools we need to fulfill what we are called to do, whether a great voice, great mind, healing spirit, we must learn from our families what that is. We are all

members of God's great family, all descendants
of Abraham through Adam and Eve, but that
doesn't mean that we don't have to fulfill our
assignment.

God raises us up to be great children of
God fulfilling our destinies. Our families help us
fulfill our destinies. Sometimes we learn from
our families what that may be, just by the family
we are born into, other times we find it out by
being on the journey.

Every one of us must fulfill our assignment
and when we don't we will suffer. Our families
are a great way to start following God's will for
us in our lives. Our families, even those that are
not the best, are a great way for us to see God
and see our assignment.

Take a Deep Breath.

Get into a comfortable position.

Breathe In through your nose for 4 counts.

Hold for 7 counts.

Breathe out through your mouth for 8 counts.

Repeat 3 times.

Matthew 3:9-10

And do not think you can say to yourselves, We have Abraham as our father.' I tell you that out of these stones God can raise up children for Abraham. The ax is already at the root of the trees, and every tree that does not produce good fruit will be cut down and thrown into the fire.

Peace I leave with you. My Peace I give you. Go in Peace. AMEN

Reflections and Final Thoughts

_____

_____

_____

_____

_____

Day 2: *Following God*

When God calls us to go and do we must
follow, we should listen and be obedient. God
calls each of us to something. When God uses us
sometimes he calls us in our families to do an
assignment. Family allegiance is important. We
should all support and uphold our families, but
when it comes to God we must put God first and
follow and listen to the call of God.

It can be very difficult to do just this but it
is so important. Many times, God will call us out
of our families to do work. God sometimes, will
call us far away from our families to complete
our assignment.

Following God and staying focused on God
doesn't mean we abandon our families. It does
mean however that to complete our assignment
we must follow God first and continue to
support our families. It is hard to cleave from all
we know and turn away from a life we are

comfortable with, but God will provide all we need. Yes, family first, but God above all else.

When God calls us to go and to leave, to cleave we must listen and obey. God will provide.

Take a Deep Breath.
Get into a comfortable position.
Breathe In through your nose for 4 counts.
Hold for 7 counts.
Breathe out through your mouth for 8 counts.
Repeat 3 times.

Matthew 4:21-22

Going on from there, he saw two brothers, James son of Zebedee and his brother John. They were in a boat with their father Zebedee, preparing their nets. Jesus called them, and immediately they left the boat and their father and followed him.

Peace I leave with you. My Peace I give you. Go in Peace. AMEN

Reflections and Final Thoughts

_____

_____

_____

_____

_____

Day 3: *Family Dynamics*

Paul had much to say regarding family. He instructs the church to act like a family. Even Jesus instructs the church to care for one another as if we are all from one big happy family. He makes sure upon his death that his favorite disciple inherits his mother even though Mary had other children.

Paul teaches that the head of the house is the father, just as God is our head. When looking as those in places of leadership Paul writes that the overseer/deacon must be able to manage his own family and have obedient children that respect him.

Managing the family well is the first step in being able to lead the family, the church in the direction it is to go. The family lays the groundwork for future leadership within the body of Christ.

When we can manage the families God's

provides for us then we can surely manage the assignment God has prepared for us.

Take a Deep Breath.

Get into a comfortable position.

Breathe In through your nose for 4 counts.

Hold for 7 counts.

Breathe out through your mouth for 8 counts.

Repeat 3 times.

1 Timothy 3:2-5

Now the overseer is to be above reproach, faithful to his wife, temperate, self-controlled, respectable, hospitable, able to teach, not given to drunkenness, not violent but gentle, not quarrelsome, not a lover of money. He must manage his own family well and see that his children obey him, and he must do so in a manner worthy of full respect. If anyone does not know how to manage his own family, how can he take care of God's church?

Peace I leave with you. My Peace I give you. Go in PEACE. AMEN

Reflections and Final Thoughts

_____

_____

_____

_____

_____

Day 4: *Honor and Respect for Parents*

Family Dynamics causes us to respect our mothers and fathers, and to also respect our elders. Family dynamics means that even when we find that our parents and elders are human and make mistakes that we should never hold that against them. Family dynamics require respect even in the bad times.

Our God requires of us God's love respect and adoration, and so do our fathers and mothers, for this is the will of God. When we find out our parents are human and make mistakes we should continue to honor them. This may mean that we distance ourselves from bad behavior, but we are born into families and from these families our assignments are prepared and perfected.

When we fail to realize that our parents make mistakes and dishonor them because of their mistakes we will find ourselves at risk to be cursed just as Ham was cursed for his actions against his father, Noah.

Our parents may not be the best adults, the best people, the best followers of Christ, they make mistakes just like we do, but God's word shows us that we must respect them as our parents even when they make mistakes. Placing God's examples at the forefront of our minds when our parents disappoint us helps us to honor them, respect them and love them with God's love.

Take a Deep Breath.
Get into a comfortable position.
Breathe In through your nose for 4 counts.
Hold for 7 counts.
Breathe out through your mouth for 8 counts.
Repeat 3 times.

Genesis 9:20-23

Noah, a man of the soil, proceeded to plant a vineyard. When he drank some of its wine, he became drunk and lay uncovered inside his tent. Ham, the father of Canaan, saw his father naked and told his two brothers outside. But Shem and Japheth took a garment and laid it across their shoulders; then they walked in backward and covered their father's naked body. Their faces were turned the other way so that they would not see their father naked.

Peace I leave with you. My Peace I give you.
Go in PEACE. AMEN.

Reflections and Final Thoughts

_____

_____

_____

_____

_____

Day 5: *Brothers and Sisters*

As Christian's we are not only born into our birth families, we also are born into the body the Christ, the eternal family. When we are born again we are born again into this great big family of God.

We hope and pray that our birth families also join this family of God, but when we are called we must heed the call and go and follow God and be grafted into the great tree of life. God gives us a larger family once we become Christians, this doesn't negate our birth families, but sometimes these church families can be stronger than our birth families.

Our birth families teach us much about who we are and what we are to do here on earth, and our Christian families help us to see that plan and follow God in all that we do. Our Christian families can be made up of all those same elements; mother, father, sister, brother.

Spiritual mothers and fathers lead us and help us to grow stronger in our faith in God. They nourish our souls and they teach us all those things that God needs for us to learn.

Our spiritual parents not only teach us, but they too learn from us. Our spiritual sisters and brothers can sometimes be our biggest cheerleaders and confidants. They hold our secrets and hold us up. They pray with us and for us, and they keep us grounded in God's love and light. Our spiritual families are gifts from God to be cherished and loved and held on to and cultivated like the gifts they are.

Take a Deep Breath.

Get into a comfortable position.

Breathe In through your nose for 4 counts.

Hold for 7 counts.

Breathe out through your mouth for 8 counts.

Repeat 3 times.

Mark 3:31-35

Then Jesus' mother and brothers arrived. Standing outside, they sent someone in to call him. A crowd was sitting around him, and they told him, "Your mother and brothers are outside looking for you." "Who are my mother and my brothers?" he asked. Then he looked at those seated in a circle around him and said, "Here are my mother and my brothers! Whoever does God's will is my brother and sister and mother?"

Peace I leave with you. My peace I give you.
Go in PEACE.   AMEN

Reflections and Final Thoughts

_____

_____

_____

_____

_____

Day 6: *Family Loyalty*

When something good or bad happens to
one person in a family it happens to all.
Families stick together and carry one another's
burdens, in the good times and the bad. As
brothers and sisters in Christ, families, we must
look out for, we must honor, we must love and
support and be there for one another. When
there is a time in our lives when something bad
happens to someone we love we all suffer in that
struggle. Whether it be a bad mistake, a bad
diagnosis, a bad habit, a bad decision we who
love that person suffer sometimes just as much
as the family member we love. We must remain
loyal to our families even in the bad times. We
must also remain loyal to God even when we
don't like what's going on, always remembering
that God doesn't forsake those whom he loves.
Being loyal to God means following God's
decrees even when we are hurting, it means

following Gods rule of love even when we don't
have any love to give. Family loyalty does mean
loving, honoring and respecting our families,
but we must put God's ultimate call of love
before all else, even in our anger, in order to
truly honor God.

Take a Deep Breath.
Get into a comfortable position.
Breathe In through your nose for 4 counts. Hold
for 7 counts.
Breathe out through your mouth for 8 counts.
Repeat 3 times.

Genesis 34:1-4; 11-12;25-27;30

*Now Dinah, the daughter Leah had borne
to Jacob, went out to visit the women of the
land. When Shechem son of Hamor the Hivite,
the ruler of that area, saw her, he took her and
raped her. His heart was drawn to Dinah
daughter of Jacob; he loved the young woman
and spoke tenderly to her. And Shechem said to
his father Hamor, "Get me this girl as my
wife." Then Shechem said to Dinah's father and
brothers, "Let me find favor in your eyes, and I
will give you whatever you ask. Make the price
for the bride and the gift I am to bring as great
as you like, and I'll pay whatever you ask me.
Only give me the young woman as my wife."*

*"Because their sister Dinah had been
defiled, Jacob's sons replied deceitfully as they
spoke to Shechem and his father Hamor"*

*Three days later, while all of them were
still in pain, two of Jacob's sons, Simeon and*

Levi, Dinah's brothers, took their swords and attacked the unsuspecting city, killing every male. They put Hamor and his son Shechem to the sword and took Dinah from Shechem's house and left. The sons of Jacob came upon the dead bodies and looted the city where their sister had been defiled. Then Jacob said to Simeon and Levi, "You have brought trouble on me by making me obnoxious to the Canaanites and Perizzites, the people living in this land. We are few in number, and if they join forces against me and attack me, I and my household will be destroyed."

Peace I leave with you. My Peace I give you.
Go in PEACE. AMEN

Reflections and Final Thoughts

_____

_____

_____

_____

_____

Day 7: One with God

When we are grafted into the tree of life with God we become one with God and one Christian family. Jesus knew this full well. Jesus, being the son of God, knew that we were all siblings, all sisters and brothers in Christ.

Being one family we are all given the same charge to preach the gospel of God to all nations. We must baptize them into God's love. Jesus wants all of us to believe this message of love and faithfulness to God. May we all be glorified in God's name. May we all be in God and have God in us.

As we meditate on God's word and hide it in our hearts so that we have the tools we need to follow God with our entire being, may we continue to seek God in all that we do. Jesus continues to make God known to each of us as God leads us. The Holy Spirit living in us, lives in all baptized believers, this bond, this connection, this link makes us all family. One family in Christ. God's love continues to grow us closer and closer and stronger in the tree of life. Let us all be one with Christ as we are one with one another.

Take a Deep Breath.
Get into a comfortable position.
Breathe In through your nose for 4 counts.
Hold for 7 counts.
Breathe out through your mouth for 8 counts.
Repeat 3 times.

John 17:20-26

My prayer is not for them alone. I pray also for those who will believe in me through their message, that all of them may be one, Father, just as you are in me and I am in you. May they also be in us so that the world may believe that you have sent me. I have given them the glory that you gave me, that they may be one as we are one— I in them and you in me—so that they may be brought to complete unity.

Then the world will know that you sent me and have loved them even as you have loved me. "Father, I want those you have given me to be with me where I am, and to see my glory, the glory you have given me because you loved me before the creation of the world. "Righteous Father, though the world does not know you, I know you, and they know that you have sent me. I have made you known to them, and will continue to make you known in order that the love you have for me may be in them and that I myself may be in them."

Peace I leave with you. My Peace I give you. Go in PEACE. AMEN.

Reflections and Final Thoughts

_____

_____

_____

_____

_____

So, the 21 days are up, now what?

You've made it. You've completed this 21-day challenge. Congratulations! Meditating God's way with God's word, hiding God's word deep in your heart, having scriptural passages that will encourage you and help you during those necessary times will be an important part of your everyday. These past 21 days we have focused on our health, wealth, and family. We have focused on scriptural passages that help us to see what God says about these important areas in our lives. We have challenged ourselves to quiet our minds to be reminded of God's word and how it relates to our everyday lives. We have completed this 21-day process.

So, what's next? I've said it takes 21 days to form a habit, but unfortunately it really only takes one day to break it, so I encourage you to keep it going. Find scriptures that are meaningful to you, take a mediation that was particularly encouraging to you and continue using this scripture in this practice of meditation. Do you have a life verse? Use that to mediate with. Did you use music in your mediation or silence? Try something different. Did you use beads? There is a wealth of information out there to continue this is process. I encourage you to find what's right for you.

The next 21 days could be used to repeat these same meditations but mix them up. Do all of Day 1, then Day 2 and so forth. Maybe use music as a calming agent and repeat them in the same order or backwards. I have also included meditations in the last section of this book, begin using these and then create your own. Meditation is not a science. Do whatever works for you. These meditative prayers help in the beginning stages of learning to meditate; they also give you God's word as tools to be used to combat any situation in life. As you learn and deepen your practice of mediation you may find that guided meditation is not for you. You may find that silence, lectio divina, mantras may work better. I encourage you to look at all these other forms of meditation as well. Once you've incorporated meditation in to your daily schedule you'll notice the change in your entire self; mind, body and spirit.

MEDITATIONS

LOVE

Let's talk about love. Love, sweet love. We all need it, we all want it, and some of us have it just the way we like it. God teaches us about love. God tell us that love is patient and kind and not envious. God loved us so much that Jesus was given to us to make atonement for our sins. This love that God has for us is not self-serving, self-seeking. This love protects the betrothed. Love sweet love does not dishonor the giver or the taker. This love is the kind of love that never leaves, never fails, never... Faith, hope and love, but the greatest of these is love. (13:13)

1 Corinthians 13:4-8a

Love is patient, love is kind. It does not envy, it does not boast, it is not proud. It does not dishonor others, it is not self-seeking, it is not easily angered, it keeps no record of wrongs. Love does not delight in evil but rejoices with the truth. It always protects, always trusts, always hopes, always perseveres. Love never fails.

Peace I leave with you. My Peace I give you. Go in Peace. Amen

Trials and Tribulations

When we face trials and tribulations the
last thing we are thinking about is joy! How can
one be joyful when they ae looking at what
seems like will destroy their very existence?
How can one put a real smile on their face in the
middle of pain and sorrow? We read that
weeping may endure for a night but joy comes
in the morning, well though the tears how can
we have joy on our minds? God's word tells us
that when we are faced with the many trials and
tribulations that we will face along our journey
that we should be joyful because God is testing
our faith. Trials and tribulations teach us to
persevere and grow our faith and strength in
the Lord. Trials and tribulations mature us in
our faith. When we trust God in the storm we
can be like Jesus when the storms of life come
raging in we can be asleep in the bottom of the

hull knowing that God's got us. When we persevere during the trials of life we are blessed, and receive all the promises God has in store for us.

James 1:2-12

Consider it pure joy, my brothers and sisters, whenever you face trials of many kinds,

because you know that the testing of your faith produces perseverance. Let perseverance finish its work so that you may be mature and complete, not lacking anything. If any of you lacks wisdom, you should ask God, who gives generously to all without finding fault, and it will be given to you.

But when you ask, you must believe and not doubt, because the one who doubts is like a wave of the sea, blown and tossed by the wind.

That person should not expect to receive anything from the Lord. Such a person is double-minded and unstable in all they do.

Believers in humble circumstances ought to take pride in their high position. But the rich should take pride in their humiliation—since they will pass away like a wild flower. For the sun rises with scorching heat and withers the plant; its blossom falls and its beauty is destroyed.

In the same way, the rich will fade away even while they go about their business. Blessed is the one who perseveres under trial because, having stood the test, that person will receive the crown of life that the Lord has promised to those who love him.

Peace I leave with you. My peace I give you. Go in peace. Amen.

Thankfulness

Thankfulness, the act of being thankful, is that a learned trait or is it something we are born with? What does it truly mean to be thankful? Can our thankfulness, or our ability to be thankful change? Being thankful in all things is something we all must cultivate in our daily walk. God has predestined our journey, and everything that happens along the way God had had God's hand in. Even in the bad things, God is there and even though we don't like how it feels, we must be thankful for this is God's will in our lives, the lives that are in Christ Jesus. God is a good and merciful God. God's loves for us, God's children, endures forever. So, when we tell our stories of redemption we must should on high exclaiming the goodness of God, the mercies of God, the love of God. Our God is good, and God is good all the time.

Psalm 107:1-3

Give thanks to the Lord, for he is good; his love endures forever. Let the redeemed of the Lord tell their story— those he redeemed from the hand of the foe, those he gathered from the lands, from east and west, from north and south.

Peace I leave with you. My peace I give you. Go in peace. Amen.

Rejoice

Rejoice, the act of rejoicing. Rejoice, showing joy and pleasure, delight and happiness. Rejoicing in the Lord every day all day seems like a daunting task, even with everyday life's circumstances, but that is where meditation comes in. When we meditate on God's word, it reminds us even in the middle of the day to rejoice in God. When we are tender and gentle and kind, like our Lord Jesus we can rejoice in all things, our anxiety is quelled because we are constantly in communion with God. God's peace lives and moves and abides within us. God's peace will guard our hearts and minds. When we guard our hearts and minds in God's hands, and think on all things worthy of praising God's name, then God's peace will rest and abide within us.

Philippians 4:4-9

Rejoice in the Lord always. I will say it again: Rejoice! Let your gentleness be evident to all. The Lord is near. Do not be anxious about anything, but in every situation, by prayer and petition, with thanksgiving, present your requests to God. And the peace of God, which transcends all understanding, will guard your hearts and your minds in Christ Jesus. Finally, brothers and sisters, whatever is true, whatever is noble, whatever is right, whatever is pure, whatever is lovely, whatever is admirable — if anything is excellent or praiseworthy— think about such things.

Whatever you have learned or received or heard from me, or seen in me — put it into practice. And the God of peace will be with you.

Peace I leave with you. My peace I give you.
Go in peace. Amen

Lament

There is a time and a place for all things. To
be honest with ourselves, and with God we must
lament. Just as there is a time to be born, as
well as a time to die, we too must lament and
cry out to God in our distress, because God will
hear us. When we are not honest with ourselves
or God how then can God help us. Yes, the goal
is to be thankful in all things, but we have to get
to the thankfulness, and lamenting is part of the
journey. When we don't lament, we can drive
ourselves insane. When we don't lament, those
feelings can just gnaw away at our insides and
tear us apart. Here the writer remembers their
afflictions, and sadness, and describes how their
soul was downcast and broken, but he doesn't
stop there in the lament. She remembers God's
great love for her and remembers that God will
be compassionate and will hear her cries if only
she waits for God. He remembers that God will

bring them out of the pit and will not allow their sadness to consume them forever. When we wait on the Lord patiently, hoping in God's deliverance God will heed and listen and answer our cries even in our distress.

Lamentations 3:19-26

I remember my affliction and my wandering, the bitterness and the gall. I well remember them, and my soul is downcast within me. Yet this I call to mind and therefore I have hope: Because of the Lord's great love we are not consumed, for his compassions never fail. They are new every morning; great is your faithfulness. I say to myself, "The Lord is my portion; therefore I will wait for him." The Lord is good to those whose hope is in him, to the one who seeks him; it is good to wait quietly for the salvation of the Lord.

Peace I leave with you. My peace I give to you.

Go in peace. Amen.

———————————————

Dr. Aliya Browne is a board certified clinical cardiologist who specializes in integrative medicine and preventive cardiovascular care and is presently in private practice at Designed 4 Wellness LLC. She received her Bachelor's degree from Temple University, and attended New York College of Osteopathic Medicine /New York Institute of Technology in Old Westbury NY, where she received her Doctor of Osteopathic Medicine. She is board certified in Internal Medicine and Cardiology. She is a licensed minister and a graduate of Princeton Theological Seminary. She is trained as a spiritual director through Oasis Ministries.

Previously in private practice at Central Jersey Heart Group LLC in Ewing, NJ, she completed a fellowship in integrative medicine at the University of Arizona Class of 2015, and a fellowship in noninvasive cardiology at Deborah Heart & Lung Center. She is passionate about caring for the total person, and integrates eastern, western and spiritual practices into one practice of integrative cardiology at Designed 4 Wellness LLC.

Dr. Browne is a sought-after lecturer, and speaker on women and heart disease, and has been featured in newspaper, magazine articles, Radio and television discussing these same issues.

Dr. Browne is happily married to her college sweetheart, and is mother to teenage twins and a eleven year old. Her motto is 'To whom much is given much is required'. She dedicates her medical career to her grandmother who died suddenly from heart disease when she was thirteen. This had a dramatic impact on her life and has guided her in her specialty path.

References

i Kabatt-Zinn, Jon, Wherever You Go There You Are. New York: Hyperion, 1994.

ii Gunaratana, Bhante, Mindfulness in Plain English. Boston: Wisdom Publications, 2014.

iii Weil, Andrew. drweil.com. Three Breathing Exercises. May 2016.

iv Merriam Webster Incorporated. Merriam-Webster Dictionary. Merriam-webster.com

9 780990 871385